A WEEK IN THE LIFE OF ME

by Amy Krouse Rosenthal

CHRONICLE BOOKS

San Francisco

ISBN 978-1-4521-3443-7

Manufactured in China
Design by Hillary Caudle

Chronicle Books publishes distinctive books and gifts.
From award-winning children's titles, bestselling cook-
books, and eclectic pop culture to acclaimed works of art
and design, stationery, and journals, we craft publishing
that's instantly recognizable for its spirit and creativity.
Enjoy our publishing and become part of our community
at www.chroniclebooks.com.

MIX
Paper from
responsible sources
FSC
www.fsc.org   FSC™ C008047

Chronicle Books LLC
680 Second Street
San Francisco, CA 94107
www.chroniclebooks.com

WELCOME TO
A WEEK IN THE LIFE OF ME.

Simply begin on any day of the week and continue for seven
consecutive days. Enjoy reflecting now and thank yourself later.

This journal is:

○ a gift from _____.

○ something I gave to myself.

I chose this week to fill it in because:

○ I wanted to do so as soon as I got it.

○ It's something I've been meaning to do for a while.

○ Now seemed like as good a time as any.

Today's date is _____,

which makes me precisely _____ years old.

Signed _____

DAY

1

○ ○ ○ ○ ○ ○ ○

DATE

LOOKING AROUND THIS ROOM,
here's what I see:

_____

_____

LOOKING OUT THE WINDOW,
here's what I see:

_____

_____

LOOKING AT THE WEEK AHEAD,
here's what I see:

_____

_____

_____

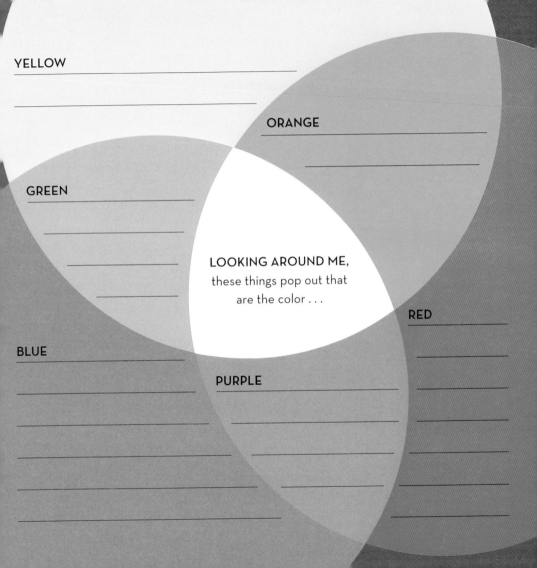

YELLOW

ORANGE

GREEN

LOOKING AROUND ME,
these things pop out that
are the color . . .

RED

BLUE

PURPLE

My address:

_____

I've lived here for:

_____

When I walk in the door, the first thing I usually do:

_____

Other humans (and nonhumans) I live with:

_____   _____

_____   _____

_____   _____

HERE'S WHERE I FALL ON THE SPECTRUM:

Hoping to move ASAP ●———+———+———+———● _Love my home so much_

Draw a line to identify each response:

My willpower •

Me, physically •

My eyesight •

My ties to old friends •

My connection with siblings •

How I like my coffee •

My sense of what I want from life •

My vocabulary •

My sense of humor •

My handshake •

• *Strong*

• *Medium*

• *Weak*

TODAY'S
FIRSTS

First person I **SAW:**

First person I **TEXTED:**

First thing I **ATE:**

First thing I **DID** at work/school:

Wish I will make on the proverbial
FIRST STAR I SEE TONIGHT:

the
FIRST THING

MONDAY

TUESDAY

WEDNESDAY

THURSDAY

FRIDAY

SATURDAY

SUNDAY

GOALS

By the end of the day today:

By the end of the week:

A wee small goal in my life right now:

A big meaningful goal in my life right now:

Goals I've recently accomplished:

When I look back on this in ten years, I hope I have:

Mark where you land on this grid:

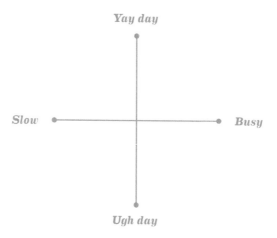

Yay day

Slow ● ──────────────── ● Busy

Ugh day

NOTE TO SELF

One thing I'd like to remember about this day:

LASTLY . . .

The last thing I was
OUT-OF-MY-MIND EXCITED ABOUT:

DAY

2

DATE

MY CURRENT
CIRCLE OF FRIENDS

Write best friends in the center; acquaintances around the periphery:

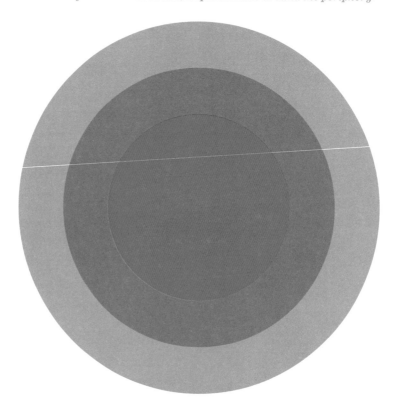

It's fair to say **I SPEND A LOT OF**
TIME . . .

Check all that apply:

- ○ in my car
- ○ at my desk
- ○ exercising
- ○ outside
- ○ procrastinating
- ○ doing dishes
- ○ doing laundry
- ○ volunteering
- ○ online
- ○ working
- ○ laughing
- ○ parenting
- ○ at a place of worship

- ○ cooking
- ○ studying
- ○ worrying
- ○ complaining
- ○ skipping
- ○ growing things in my garden
- ○ growing as a person
- ○ talking
- ○ listening
- ○ other:

_____

_____

MAKING SENSE OF MY LIFE THROUGH MY SENSES:

SCENT(S) in the air:

Footsteps I always immediately recognize:

SOUNDS I hear:

What's in my bag:

TASTE in my mouth:

A sight that makes my heart beat faster:

Opening the fridge, here's what I see:

My fridge right now is:

○ clean and organized

○ a mess

○ jam-packed

○ sadly bare

○ full of home-cooked leftovers

○ full of take-out cartons

What's tacked to outside of fridge:

BOOKS

Book(s) I'm reading **NOW:**

Recent book(s) I've **LOVED:**

Book(s) I'm thinking about reading **NEXT:**

Author I'd really like to meet:

I seem to read most of my books:

○ digitally
○ in hardcover or paperback
○ in bed
○ on transit

MY DESERT ISLAND BOOKSHELF

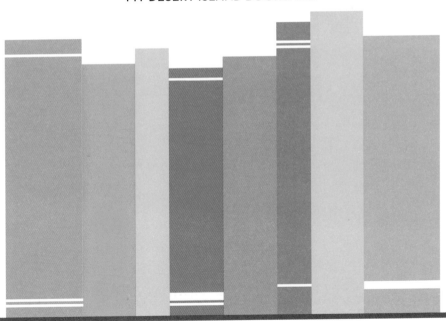

Write book titles on spines.

What I woke up to this morning:
- ○ alarm clock
- ○ phone alarm
- ○ this song:

_____

- ○ slept 'til I woke up

WHAT'S ON MY NIGHTSTAND

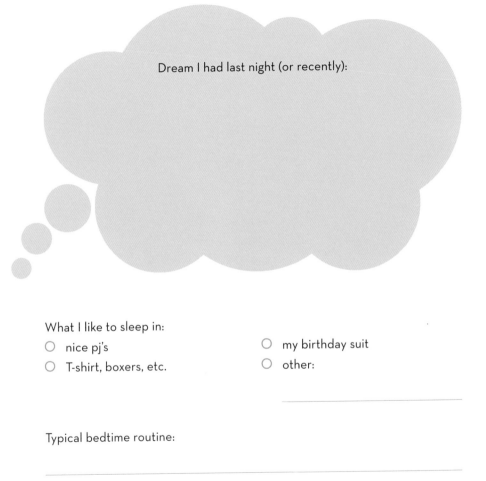

Dream I had last night (or recently):

What I like to sleep in:
○ nice pj's
○ T-shirt, boxers, etc.
○ my birthday suit
○ other:

_____

Typical bedtime routine:

_____

_____

Mark where you land on this grid:

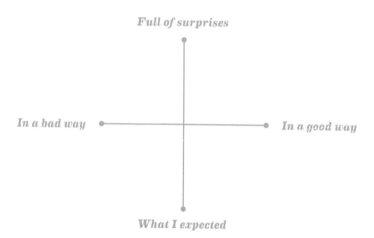

Full of surprises

In a bad way

In a good way

What I expected

NOTE TO SELF
One thing I'd like to remember about this day:

LASTLY . . .

The last time I
LAUGHED MY HEAD OFF:

_____

_____

_____

_____

_____

_____

_____

_____

_____

DAY

3

●●●○○○○

DATE

GREATER THAN /
LESS THAN

Fill in with a > or < sign to indicate which you prefer:

THIS	is greater than/less than	THIS
	> <	
staying home	_____	going out
small dinner party	_____	hitting the clubs
city	_____	country
lake	_____	ocean
coffee	_____	tea
shower	_____	bath
traditional	_____	modern
winter	_____	summer
cooking	_____	ordering in

going to bed early	___	staying up late
scrambled	___	fried
busy	___	lazy
dogs	___	cats
giving	___	receiving
truth	___	dare
being in sweats	___	getting dressed up
familiar routine	___	shaking things up

Lately, I'm
SUPER OBSESSED
with: _____

_____

FAMILY

MY FAMILY PORTRAIT

Draw inside the frame.

My parents currently live _____ miles away.

I would like to live:
- ○ closer to family
- ○ farther away from family
- ○ as is—it feels perfect

Friends that feel like family:

_____

_____

Family member that I go to for advice:

_____

I should really call: _____

Because: _____

Looking at my phone's camera roll, you will see a lot of the following . . .

PEOPLE:

PLACES:

FOODS:

I can't seem to stop taking photos of:

THE LAST THREE PHOTOS I POSTED ONLINE:

Photo   *Where I posted it*

EMBARRASSING PHOTO WORTH A GOOD LAUGH:

Check all that apply:

overwhelmed ○	content ○	grateful ○
peaceful ○	unhappy ○	brave ○
confused ○	tired ○	happy to be alive ○
rushed ○	hungover ○	psyched ○
inspired ○	melancholy ○	concerned ○
healthy and fit ○	scattered ○	giddy ○
anxious ○	focused ○	hopeful ○

Allow me to elaborate a bit:

Mark where you land on this grid:

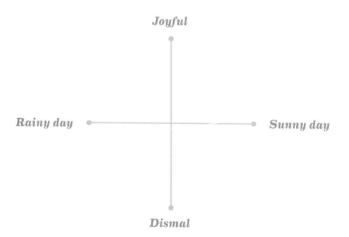

Joyful

Rainy day — — — — *Sunny day*

Dismal

NOTE TO SELF
One thing I'd like to remember about this day:

The last thing I
CRIED ABOUT:

DAY

4

●●●●○○○

DATE

IF I COULD FREEZE
A MOMENT IN TIME

My day, roughly by the hour

12 AM _____	12 PM _____
1 AM _____	1 PM _____
2 AM _____	2 PM _____
3 AM _____	3 PM _____
4 AM _____	4 PM _____
5 AM _____	5 PM _____
6 AM _____	6 PM _____
7 AM _____	7 PM _____
8 AM _____	8 PM _____
9 AM _____	9 PM _____
10 AM _____	10 PM _____
11 AM _____	11 PM _____

TO DO

On my current to-do list:

_____

_____

_____

On my calendar for the week:

_____

_____

_____

Errands I need to run:

_____

_____

_____

THIS WEEK'S
BEST

FRIEND	CONVERSATION
NEWS	DECISION
RESTAURANT OR MEAL	MOMENT

FRIEND

CONVERSATION

NEWS

DECISION

RESTAURANT OR MEAL

MOMENT

MUSIC

♪ **SONGS/BANDS** I'm loving:

♪ Last **LIVE MUSIC** show I've seen:

♪ **ALBUM** I recently discovered:

♪ An artist everyone loves but I am just **NOT FEELING IT:**

♪ **GUILTY PLEASURE:**

♪ **RADIO STATION(S)** of choice:

MY PLAYLIST *of the*
WEEK

Song 1

Song 2

Song 3

Song 4

Song 5

Song 6

Song 7

TRAVEL
WISHLIST

CITIES/COUNTRIES:

_____

_____

_____

_____

_____

_____

_____

_____

_____

ZOOMING IN

on one of the aforementioned:

_____

_____

_____

_____

_____

_____

_____

_____

_____

Mark where you land on this grid:

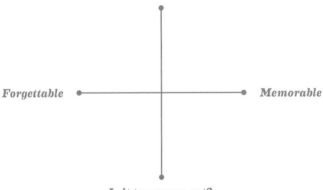

Wish this day would last forever

Forgettable ●————————————————● *Memorable*

Is it tomorrow yet?

NOTE TO SELF
One thing I'd like to remember about this day:

_____

_____

The last thing I
TREATED MYSELF TO:

_____

_____

_____

_____

_____

_____

_____

_____

_____

DAY

5

DATE

LET'S
FACE IT

MY HAIRSTYLE
Draw in.

WHAT'S ON MY MIND:

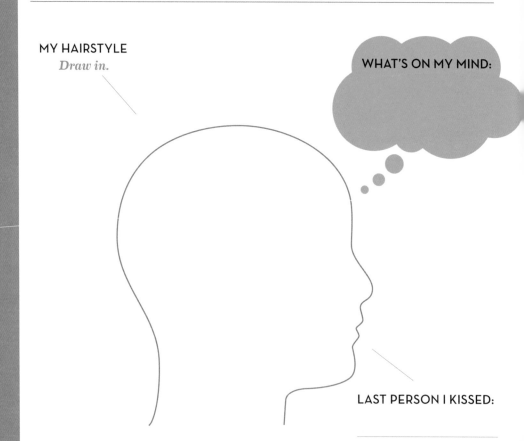

LAST PERSON I KISSED:

A few of my favorite hobbies:

_____

_____

Last hobby I picked up:

_____

_____

Something I'd like to try:

_____

_____

CLOTHES

Here's a rough sketch of what I'm wearing now:

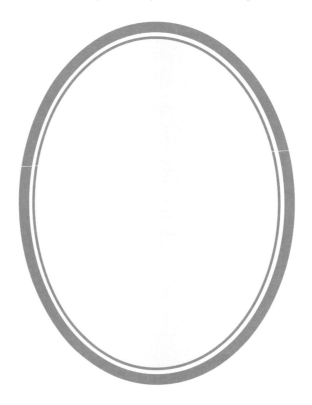

Items of clothing I seem to wear the most:

_____

_____

_____

Favorite recent purchase:

_____

_____

Best shoes ever:

_____

_____

My closet is:
- ○ a mess
- ○ totally tidy and organized
- ○ overflowing; need to give some things away
- ○ looking rather sparse
- ○ not something I think about that much

Recent movie(s) I **LOVED:**

Movie I'm **HIGHLY ANTICIPATING:**

LAST MOVIE I SAW in a theater:

Who I'd cast as **ME** in the movie of my life:

My favorite
VIRAL VIDEO: ....

TELEVISION

TV SHOWS I am really digging these days:

Recent **BINGES** of entire seasons include:

I prefer watching:
- ○ on my computer/tablet
- ○ on my phone
- ○ on my old-school big screen

A **TELEVISION CHARACTER**
that really seems to be staying with me:

SLANG I'M USING, YO

Mark where you land on this grid:

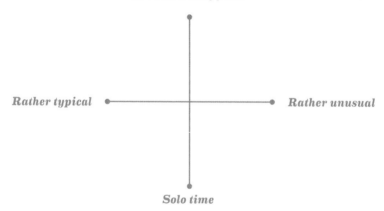

Around a lot of folks

Rather typical — — — — *Rather unusual*

Solo time

NOTE TO SELF
One thing I'd like to remember about this day:

_____

_____

The last time I felt
PRETTY DARN PROUD OF MYSELF:

_____

_____

_____

_____

_____

_____

_____

_____

_____

_____

DAY

6

●●●●●● ○

DATE

Dear _____ ,

Thank you for . . .

_____

_____

_____

_____

_____

_____

_____

_____

_____

Dear _____,

Just a note to say . . .

_____

_____

_____

_____

_____

_____

_____

HOLIDAYS

Holiday coming up that I'm looking forward to:

Favorite holiday traditions:

Crazy holiday story:

Spirituality to me means:

RANDOM
CHECK

Check all that apply:

☐ I often pick up the check

☐ I get regular checkups

☐ I have a book checked out from the library

☐ I am always checking out new things

☐ I've been to the Czech Republic

☐ I pay my bills by writing a check

☐ When I get in front of a microphone I tend to say "check, check"

MY
PHONE

My cell #:

My current phone model:

_____

_____

Who's paying the bill:

_____

The app(s) I'm using a lot these days:

_____

_____

MY PHONE IS WITH ME:

Never o———————+———————+———————+———————o *Always*

The last four people I texted:

_____   _____

_____   _____

I'll transcribe a message or two here:

The last three people I spoke to
voice-to-voice:

_____

_____

_____

yes, I HAVE A LANDLINE.
○

WHAT'S A LANDLINE?
○

CLUBS
I'M A PART OF

[Books, movies, games, churches, etc.]

BY THE
NUMBERS

Insert your numbers:

_____ = hours of sleep I get most nights

_____ = glasses of water I drink daily

_____ = hours I work per day

_____ = hours I spend each day online

_____ = time I plop down on the couch each night

_____ = minutes I can stay focused

_____ = number of pounds I fluctuate

_____ = size of my ideal family

_____ = minutes a day I spend: _____

Mark where you land on this grid:

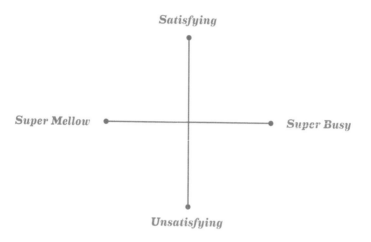

Satisfying

Super Mellow

Super Busy

Unsatisfying

NOTE TO SELF
One thing I'd like to remember about this day:

LASTLY . . .

The last
MOMENT OF TOTAL RELAXATION
I remember:

_____

_____

_____

_____

_____

_____

_____

_____

DAY

7

DATE

60 SECONDS.
GO!

FAVORITE:

GAME

QUOTE

WORD

DREAM:

VACATION

JOB

HOUSE

MOST:

PROUD ACCOMPLISHMENT

LIKELY TO

EMBARRASSING MOMENT

KICK:

THIS HABIT

BACK AND RELAX MEANS

-ASS PERSON IN MY LIFE

FINISH THESE
SENTENCES

I'm looking forward to: _____

_____

I so love it when: _____

_____

_____

I still don't know how to: _____

_____

I've really been meaning to: _____

_____

_____

The mistake I seem to make over and over is: _____

_____

I honestly cannot believe: _____

_____

_____

People who know me well say: _____

_____

I am hopeful about: _____

_____

_____

The last person I said **"I LOVE YOU"** to: _____

The last person who said "I love you" to me:

_____

Someone who maybe doesn't know I love her/him:

_____

Lately, I feel especially **LOVED AND APPRECIATED** by:

_____

Who I'd love to see more of:

_____

Favorite love song(s):

_____

People I just **LOVE** being around:

My love life at the moment, in a nutshell:

Mark where you land on this grid:

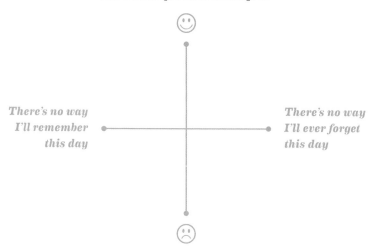

*There's no way
I'll remember
this day*

*There's no way
I'll ever forget
this day*

NOTE TO SELF

One thing I'd like to remember about this day:

LASTLY . . .

THE LAST WORD
for this week:

AND THAT CONCLUDES

A
WEEK
IN THE
LIFE
OF ME

P.S.

_____

_____

_____

P.P.S. Keep this journal in an easy-to-remember spot!